Thomas Jefferson

Jill K. Mulhall, M. Ed.

Table of Contents

Thomas Jefferson

A Great American

As a young man, Thomas Jefferson became interested in **politics**. He believed that all people had a right to freedom. He worked to make this true in America. Jefferson wrote the Declaration of Independence. Then, he helped to make laws that gave people more rights. Later, he held many important **government** jobs. Jefferson helped make the United States a great new country.

Boyhood on the Plantation

A lucky little boy was born in Virginia on April 13, 1743. His name was Thomas Jefferson. Jefferson was lucky because his family lived on a beautiful **plantation** called Shadwell. There was lots of land for him to explore. He rode horses and learned to hunt. He loved the outdoors.

Jefferson was also lucky because he had an excellent mind. He loved to learn. His family hired tutors for him. He read many books each day. He could read in five languages!

▼ Jefferson's father was a well-known surveyor in Virginia. He would have used tools like these to map the land around Shadwell.

▼ Jefferson's home was in the colony of Virginia, which is shown on this 1751 map drawn by Jefferson's father, Peter.

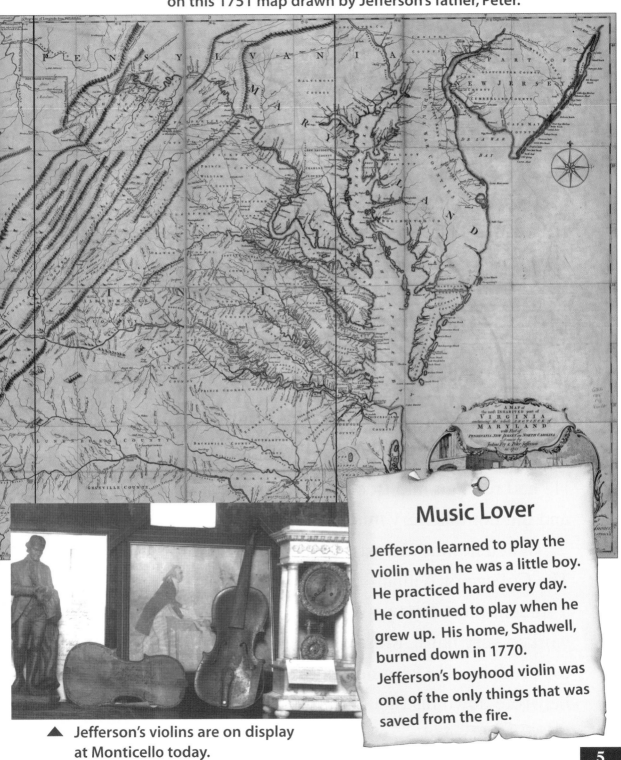

▲ Jefferson's violins are on display at Monticello today.

Music Lover

Jefferson learned to play the violin when he was a little boy. He practiced hard every day. He continued to play when he grew up. His home, Shadwell, burned down in 1770. Jefferson's boyhood violin was one of the only things that was saved from the fire.

The colonial Virginia capitol building in Williamsburg ▲

Off to College

Jefferson grew up to be tall and thin. He had red hair and freckles. He was shy and did not talk very much.

When he was almost 17, he went off to The College of William and Mary. He was a student there for two years. Jefferson worked very hard. Most days he studied for 14 hours. He kept notebooks where he wrote down his thoughts about all the things he learned.

The college was in a town called Williamsburg. It was the capital of Virginia. Many important men lived there or came to visit. Jefferson became friends with some of them. He learned by listening to them speak.

▼ The Wren Building, where Jefferson lived during college

An Early Inspiration

Many men influenced Jefferson during his years in Williamsburg. He was always grateful to his teachers of that time. Also, he was inspired by a man named Patrick Henry. Henry was well known for giving fiery speeches. Jefferson witnessed one of Henry's speeches. He remembered it for the rest of his life.

Life as a Lawyer

After college, Jefferson studied law for five years. Then, he became a lawyer. He traveled all over Virginia. He liked meeting different kinds of people.

Jefferson had lots of interests besides the law. In fact, it was hard to find a subject that did not interest him! He collected books about many different subjects. He especially loved to read about history, science, nature, and politics.

This sketch of ▶
a macaroni
machine
illustrates
Jefferson's
curious mind.

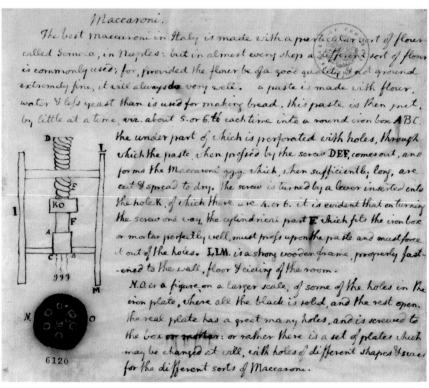

Brrrrr!

Jefferson needed long days to do all the things he wanted to do. So, he got up very early in the morning. He had a trick to help himself wake up quickly. He would stick his feet in a bucket of cold water. What a way to start the day!

Many Virginians were unhappy with their leaders in Great Britain. They did not like being told what to do by a king who lived so far away. Jefferson thought that the people should be able to make their own laws. He wrote about this in booklets and newspaper articles.

▼ This British cartoon shows Great Britain being torn in many different directions.

King George III

Working for More Freedom

The people of Virginia **elected** Jefferson to the House of Burgesses (BURR-juhs-uhs). This was the group of men who made the laws in the colony.

Jefferson worked hard. He argued for more rights for the people. He helped pass a special **resolution**. It said that Great Britain could not tax the people of Virginia. He also helped organize a **boycott** of British goods.

▼ Jefferson meeting with the Virginia Committee of Correspondence

▼ This page from Jefferson's autobiography discusses his marriage and the Committees of Correspondence.

He knew the colonies would have more power if they worked together. So, he helped begin the **Committees of Correspondence**. These groups of men wrote letters to leaders in other colonies.

Jefferson was happy to be doing such important work. Something else made him happy, too. On New Year's Day 1772, he married a woman named Martha Skelton.

Home Sweet Home

Jefferson loved **architecture** (AR-kuh-tek-chuhr). When he was 27 he designed a house for himself. He called the mansion *Monticello*. That word is Italian for "little mountain." Jefferson loved his home. He worked hard all his life to make it a unique place.

Thomas Jefferson

▲ Jefferson's home, Monticello, in Virginia

A Meeting He Would Not Miss

In 1775, the colonies went to war with Great Britain. **Delegates** went to Philadelphia for the Second **Continental** (kon-tuh-NEN-tuhl) **Congress**. This meeting would help the people decide what to do next.

Jefferson had missed the First Continental Congress. He had been too sick to travel. This time, however, he was able to go.

The delegates **debated** for many months. Some of them wanted to stay loyal to the king. Others, like Jefferson, wanted to declare **independence**.

Finally, the Congress decided to prepare a paper. It would tell the world that the colonies were now free of Great Britain. The men knew that Jefferson was a gifted writer. They chose him to write the **Declaration** (dek-luh-RAY-shuhn).

▼ Meeting of the First Continental Congress

Family Matters

It was hard for Jefferson to leave Virginia. His family was going through a sad time. His three-year-old daughter and his mother had recently died. Jefferson's wife, Martha, was very sick. He wanted to be home to take care of her.

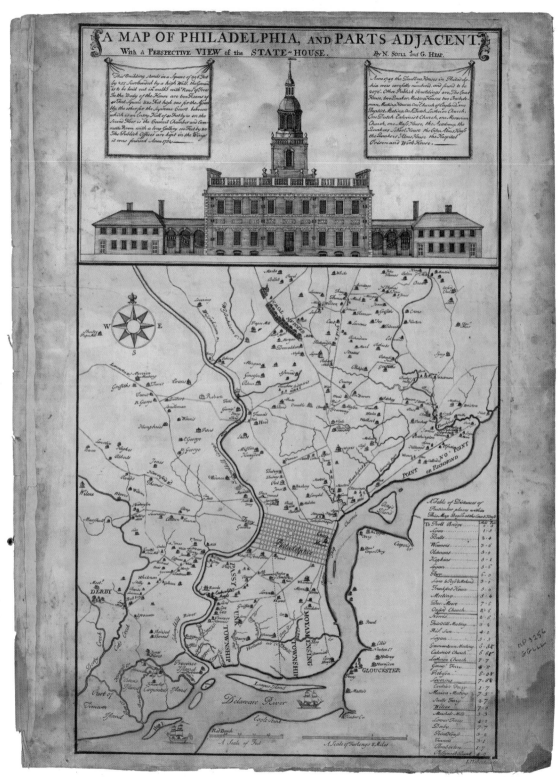

▲ This is a map of Philadelphia showing the building where the Continental Congress met.

Words That Changed the World

The Declaration was not long. But, writing it was a big job. It took Jefferson more than two weeks.

First, Jefferson described a good government. It would help people with "life, liberty, and the **pursuit** of happiness." Then, he wrote that the king had not done a good job. He had kept

▼ Jefferson and Benjamin Franklin review a draft of the Declaration of Independence.

Better on Paper

When Jefferson was young he wanted to become a great speaker. He practiced giving speeches in front of a mirror. But his voice was too soft. He was not exciting to watch. So he became known for his writing instead.

the people from making decisions about their own lives. Finally, Jefferson wrote that the colonists would no longer be British **citizens** (SIT-uh-zuhns). Instead, they would form a new country called the United States of America.

Congress liked Jefferson's work. It approved the Declaration of Independence on July 4, 1776. Jefferson was proud to have written such an important paper.

Setting Up the New Virginia

Jefferson returned home as soon as he could. He had work to do in Virginia. The colony was no longer ruled by Great Britain. So it would need a new government of its own.

For three years Jefferson wrote laws and worked to get them passed. Only people who owned land were allowed to vote. He helped change the rules so that more people could own land. This let more people to have a say in the government.

Another law he wrote gave people the right to choose their own religion. It also stated that the churches would not get money from taxes.

In 1779, the people of Virginia elected Jefferson as their governor. He served as governor for two years.

Jefferson lived in the ▶ Governor's Palace in Williamsburg, during his two years in office.

Education for Everyone

In Jefferson's time there were no public schools. People had to hire their own teachers. Jefferson thought everyone should get an education. He wrote a law calling for free schools for all children. Sadly, he could not get this law passed.

▲ Jefferson proposed many freedoms for people, such as the right to have education and freedom of religion. This document supports religious freedom.

Serving His Country

Jefferson was relieved when his term as governor was over. He wanted to stop working and spend time at Monticello with his family. But in 1782, his beloved wife Martha died. He was sick with grief. He stayed in his room for three weeks.

▼ Jefferson serving as secretary of state for President George Washington

Jefferson was no longer happy at home. So, he decided to go back to work. He returned to Congress to help organize the new country. He came up with the idea to base the United States **currency** (KUHR-uhn-see), or money, on a decimal system.

In 1784, Congress asked Jefferson to go to France. He was sent to ask other countries to trade with the United States. He sailed to Paris and stayed there for five years. It was a happy time for him.

When Jefferson returned, many things had changed. The country had a new **Constitution** and its first president. George Washington asked Jefferson to be the first secretary of state. This put Jefferson in charge of how the country dealt with other nations.

A Bitter Disagreement

Alexander Hamilton was the first secretary of the treasury. He thought that the federal government should have a lot of power. Jefferson disagreed. He thought that the people and the states should have the power. They had many arguments about this.

◀ Jefferson's calling card as minister to France

▼ The signature page of the Louisiana Purchase agreement and the case that protected it

▼ Napoleon Bonaparte, ruler of France

One Last Job

Jefferson ran for president in 1796. He lost to John Adams. Back then, the person who came in second in an election became the vice president. It did not matter whether the two agreed about things. So, Jefferson became vice president.

In 1800, Jefferson beat Adams in the election. He became the third president of the United States. He was the first president who was sworn into office in the new capital city of Washington. Jefferson was president for eight years.

In 1803, President Jefferson made a great deal. France had a huge piece of land in America. It was called the Louisiana Territory (TER-uh-tore-ee). The French leader, Napoleon Bonaparte, agreed to sell it to the United States for 15 million dollars. Overnight, the country became twice as big!

A Strange Relationship

Jefferson and Adams worked on the Declaration of Independence together. They became good friends. Later they became political rivals. In old age they became friends again. They wrote each other hundreds of letters. Both men died on the exact same day.

John Adams

Busy Final Years

In 1809, Jefferson returned home to Monticello. Many people came to visit him. Sometimes he had as many as 50 houseguests.

Jefferson filled his home with inventions. He made a machine that copied a letter as he wrote it. He experimented with new kinds of farm tools. He also built a dumbwaiter. This was a small elevator that moved food from one floor to another.

The Library of Congress burned down in 1814. Jefferson sold Congress his collection of 6,487 books to give the Library a new start. Then he kept right on buying more books. He wrote, "I cannot live without books."

▲ Jefferson's machine that copied letters

Saying One Thing, Doing Another

Jefferson fought against slavery throughout his life. He knew it was terrible. Yet he owned many slaves himself. He may have even had children with one of his slaves, Sally Hemings. Even today we do not understand this. If he knew slavery was wrong, why did he own slaves?

Jefferson still believed in public education. So, he convinced Virginia to open a state university. He designed the buildings and chose the teachers. He planned what kind of classes the school would have. He was very proud of the University of Virginia.

Thomas Jefferson lived for exactly 50 years after his famous Declaration was approved. He died on July 4, 1826. He will always be remembered as one of the important men who brought freedom to the people of the United States.

▼ **The University of Virginia**

Glossary

architecture—the art and science of designing buildings

boycott—to stop buying or using something

citizens—people who are loyal to a country and receive protection from it in return

Committees of Correspondence—groups of men from different colonies that wrote letters to one another hoping to pull the colonies together against Britain

constitution—document that outlines the laws that govern a country

Continental Congress—government meetings of the colonists in America

currency—a system of money

debated—talked about both sides of an issue

declaration—a formal announcement

delegates—people who are sent to a meeting to speak for a larger group of people

elected—chosen by voters

federal—having to do with the main central government instead of the state organizations

government—the people and organizations that run a country

independence—standing on your own, without help from anyone

plantation—a large farm on which crops are raised

politics—the ways in which governments and leaders do their work

pursuit—chasing after

resolution—a formal statement of opinion

surveyor—someone who studies and measures land